GLAS
DIALECT

A Selection of Glaswegian
Words and Anecdotes

by
Kate Sanderson

BRADWELL
BOOKS

Published by Bradwell Books
9 Orgreave Close Sheffield S13 9NP
Email: books@bradwellbooks.co.uk

© Kate Sanderson 2014

British Library Cataloguing in Publication Data:
a catalogue record for this book is available from the
British Library.

1st Edition

ISBN: 9781902674766

Print: Gomer Press, Llandysul, Ceredigion SA44 4JL

Artwork and design by: Andrew Caffrey

PHOTOGRAPH CREDITS:

GLASWEGIAN DIALECT

by Kate Sanderson

ACKNOWLEDGEMENTS

I would like to thank the staff at the People's Palace, the Riverside Museum and the Willow Tea Rooms, the Glasgow School of Art students, Tricia Lennan, Alasdair Sinclair, Val Telfer, and everyone who kindly shared their memories of Glasgow with me. A special thank you to The Glasgow Herald and Times Group for permission to use photographs from their archives and also to John Morrison of The Corolla Ice Cream Company Ltd, Ewen G. Donaldson of Glasgow Botanic Gardens, and the Lennan family who all kindly gave permission for their photographs to be published in this book.

This book is dedicated to my wee bother **Herby Lennan** (1956–2012) who sadly passed away before it was completed.

Introduction

I still belong to Glasgow despite not having lived there for a good wee while and every time I step off the train at the Central Station or Queen Street, Glasgow belongs to me once again. In spite of cosmetic changes such as the colour of George Square, new buildings and roads, Glasgow remains the same, as it's the people who make Glasgow, just as the city's slogan so aptly declares.

Glasgow is a friendly place where people speak to you on buses and, if you ask directions, they are more than willing to help. A sense of humour runs through their conversation, often in the form of a story, mostly told in a very serious manner.

Don't be offended if you are called **'hen'** or confused when told **'C'moan, get aff'** when it's time for you to get off the bus. If it's a **stoater of a day**, try a **pokey hat** and when your **drookit**, **a wee hauf** or a **wee cuppa tea** will soon cheer you up. You may prefer **a fish supper** and a **bottle of ginger** but under no circumstances do you want a **Glesga kiss**!

This wee book just gives you a flavour of a place that was the 'Second City of the Empire' and is still a vibrant and friendly place, proud of its history, and mad about shopping, football and music.

Fàilte gu Glaschu.
Kate Sanderson

The Armorial Bearings of The City of Glasgow Council

*Here is the **BIRD** that never flew*
*Here is the **TREE** that never grew*
*Here is the **BELL** that never rang*
*Here is the **FISH** that never swam*

The **BIRD** was a dead robin that was restored to life when St Mungo held it in his hands and prayed. The oak **TREE** was originally shown as a hazel branch. St Mungo was left in charge of the holy fire but fell asleep and awoke to find the fire had gone out. He collected some frozen hazel branches and when he prayed they burst into flames. The original **BELL** was said to have been given to St Mungo by the Pope but what happened to it is uncertain. In 1641 a replacement bell was purchased by the magistrates and this is now in the People's Palace. The **FISH** is a salmon with a ring in its mouth. Queen Languoreth gave her ring to a knight and Hydderch Hael, the King of Cadzow was unhappy about this so he removed the ring from the knight's finger when he was asleep and threw it into the River Clyde. The King then asked the Queen to produce the ring but, of course, she couldn't. The knight, who feared for the Queen, asked for St Mungo's help and he sent a monk to fish in the river and the ring was found in the mouth of the fish.

'Lord, let Glasgow flourish through the preaching of thy word and the praising of thy name' was inscribed on the bell of the Tron Church in 1631 and a shortened version, *'Let Glasgow Flourish'*, has been the City Motto since 1866.

Provand's Lordship, the oldest house in Glasgow
Shutterstock ©ArTono

A

A – of

Aff – off

Affa – awfully

Ah – I

Ahmur – I am

Ahmurny – I am not

Ain – own

Airn – iron (metal)

Affrontit – embarrassed

Alang – along

Alwiz – always

Amang – amongst

Amn't Ah? – Am I not?
Often used at the end of sentences
for confirmation. *Am right, amn't Ah?*

Are ye right? – Are you ready?

Arnae – aren't

Auld – old

Aw, Awe – all

Awfy – awful

Away a place – dead

Aye – yes, always

B

Babes, The – excellent, probably from 'Babes in the Wood' being rhyming slang for good

Baccy – tobacco

Backa – behind, except when it is time and it means after as in 'The backa eight': just after eight but before half past

Backside furrit – inside out, back to front

Badness – spite

Baggies – minnows

Bahookie – backside, bottom

Baith – both

Baltic – very cold; 'pure Baltic' means extremely cold

Bammy – daft

Bampot – insane, unstable nature

Banjoed – punched, getting hit

Bar L – Barlinnie Prison

Barra – barrow

Barras – famous market in Glasgow

Bashed – mashed, as in bashed neeps

Baw – ball

Bawbee – halfpenny

Bazooka'd – drunk

Beamer – red face, blushing with embarrassment

Beat it – go away

Bedraggled – in a terrible condition

Bee wan – head off in another direction

Beezer – good, great

Belong to – come from, also used to show ownership as in *'Who belongs to this scarf?'*

Belter – really good; a good-looking person

Ben – in

Bender – heavy drinking session

Bender mender – hangover cure, probably a stiff drink

Bevvy – alcoholic drink

Bide – stay

Big – most important, big school being the secondary school

Big hoose – prison

Big picture – the main feature at the cinema

Bile – boil

Bingo bus – police van

Birlin' – turning round and round, spinning, drunk

Black Mariah – the big black police bus/van

Bladdered – drunk

Blast – a portion of food or drink

Blether – gossip, chat

Blitzed – drunk

Bloodsucker – earthworm, mainly used by children

Blootered – drunk

Blotto – drunk

Boggin – very dirty, filthy

Bonce – head

Bonnie – pretty

Borra – borrow

Bother – trouble

Brammed-up – dressed up

Brassneck it – try to get way with doing something that you know is wrong

Braw – nice, good

Bubble – cry, weep

Bucket – throw out

Budgies – wearing socks over tracksuit bottoms

Bump – steal, swindle, defraud, dismissal from work

Bunnit – flat cloth cap

Burny – hot to the touch or taste

Buroo – Employment Exchange, Job Centre, Social Security

Byraway – by the way – often used at the end of sentences or even at the beginning

C

Cairt – cart

Cally dosh – money

Cannae – can't

Cannae be arsed – can't be bothered

Cargo – purchases of alcoholic drink, carry oot

Carry on – fun, good time, a lot of coming and going to sort something out

Carry oot – alcoholic drink bought from a shop to take home or to a party

Cauld – cold

Caw – to swing or turn the rope in a skipping game

Chap the door – knock on the door

Cheers – used as a greeting instead of hello and goodbye

Chib – a weapon such as a razor or a knife

Chib mark – a scar from a knife or razor

Chippie – fish and chip shop

Chokin' – very thirsty

Chuck – to give up what you are doing, to finish with a girl/boyfriend

Chuffed – very pleased

Claes – clothes

Clamp it – be quiet

Clarty – muddy, dirty

Clockwork Orange – Glasgow's Underground Railway, the Subway

Clootie – cloth

Close – entrance to a tenement – 'Dae ye live up a close?'

Cludgie – toilet

Clype – to tell on someone, tell lies

C'moan – come on

Coal-carry – piggyback

Coo – cow

Couldnae – couldn't

Couped out – flat out, asleep, unconscious

Coupon – face

Crabbit – bad tempered, grumpy

Crash ahead – get on with a job in a hurry

Cratur – creature

Crawbag – coward

Creel – wicker basket

Cuppa – cup of

D

Da – dad, father

Dabbity – transfer, a design on a piece of paper that transfers to the skin, mostly used by children

Dae – do

Damage – injure

Dauner – a short walk, saunter

Deck – hit someone hard and knock them down

Deed – dead

Didnae – didn't

Dinnae – don't

Ding – dent

Disnae – doesn't

Dizzy – being stood up on a date

Doaty – forgetful

Doesnae – doesn't

Dog school – play truant

Doof – to hit with the fist

Doon – down

Dout – cigarette end

Drag – a puff of a cigarette

Dreep – to lower yourself from a wall/roof and then drop to the ground

Dreich – usually about weather, meaning a miserable sort of day

Drookit – soaked through, usually with rain

Droont – drowned, soaked through with rain

Dug – dog

Dummy – baby's soother

Dumps – thumps on a child's back on their birthday, usually by other children – one for every year

Dumpie – short overweight person

Dundy money – redundancy pay

E

Edgie – keep a look out

Eejit – idiot

Efter – after

Efternin – afternoon

Eh, no? – isn't that right, often used as confirmation at the end of a sentence

Embra – Edinburgh

Emdy – anybody

Ender – the child who holds the end of the skipping rope; the end slice of a loaf of bread

F

Face like fizz – a very angry face

Fae – from

Fag – cigarette

Fair Monday – the first Monday of the Glasgow Fair holiday

Faither – father

Falsers – false teeth, dentures

Fancy wumman – mistress

Fankled – muddled, tangled, knotted,
  '*Ma knitting wool's aw fankled.*'

Feart – afraid, scared, frightened

Fine well – exactly, '*You know fine well whit Ah'm saying.*'

Fish supper – fish and chips

Fitba' – football

Flakie – temper tantrum

Flier, to take a – to trip up

Fling – throw

Flooer – flower

Flyman – conman, someone not to be trusted
Follie – follow
For the off – about to leave, depart, die
Frae – from
Fur – for

G

Gallus – self-assured, cheeky, full of themselves
Gammy – false, artificial
Gaun, Gawn – go, going
Gauny, Gawny – going to
Gawk – stare
Geeza – give me, let me have
Geezabrek – give me another chance, get off my case
Get crackin' – get on with it, get started
Get tore in – to do something energetically; to get tore into someone is to give them a good telling off
Gibberin' – talking nonsense
Gie – give
Ginger – not just ginger beer but any type of fizzy drink
Gink – smell
Girn – moan, whine
Glabber – mud
Glaikit – silly, stupid
Glesga kiss – head-butt

Gloamin' – twilight

Globe – light bulb

Gonnae geeza us a haun – please help me

Gonnae no dae that – Don't do that

Go your dinger – to be very annoyed

Go your duster – to work in a frantic manner, to be very annoyed

Green Lady – Health Visitor

Greese – fat from cooking; *'wi'oot the greese'* can mean a less fatty product

Greet – cry, weep

Greetin' face – someone who constantly moans

Growlers – sausages

Grun – ground

Gubbin' – thrashing

Guid – good

H

Hadnae – had not

Hairy fit – apoplectic with anger

Hame – home

Hameldaeme – the place to say when holidaying at home

Haud – hold

Haud the bus – wait a minute

Hauf – half, a measure of whisky

Haun – hand

Heave, the – to get rid of someone or something you no longer want

Hee-haw – nothing at all

Heid – head

Heider – to head the ball

Hen – affectionate term used when speaking to females; love, dear

High heid yin – person in charge

Hingin' – unwell, under the weather

Hingin' aboot with – dating a girl/boyfriend

Hoachin' – infested, very busy

Hooch aye – maybe

Hoose – house

How – often used instead of why –
'How no?' means *'Why not?'*

Howlin'– smelly

How's it gaun? – How are you getting on? – used as a greeting

Hud – had

Hunkers – haunches

Hunner – hundred

Hurl – ride in a car

Husnae – hasn't

Huv, Hud – have, had

Huvtae – have to

I

Intae – into

Intit no? – Isn't it not? – added to the end of a sentence for confirmation

Isnae – isn't

It does so – Yes it does, without doubt; used when a fact may be disputed.

J

Jag – vaccination, sharp prick

Jaiket – jacket

Jammy dodger – a very lucky person

Janny – school caretaker

Jeely – jam, jelly preserve

Jeely piece – jam or jelly sandwich

Jiggin' – dancing

Jist – just

Jooks – trousers

Jorrie – glass marble

Jotters – school exercise books; to be given yer jotters means to be sacked

Jumpin' – very angry

Just efter – just had;

'Ah'm just efter my breakfast.'

K

Keeker – black eye
Keep edgy – keep a lookout
Kegs – trousers
Ken – know
Keys! – truce in a children's game
Keys up – thumbs up
Kick yer ain arse – kick yourself
Kiddin' – joking
Kiltie – man wearing a kilt
Kin – can
Kipper's knickers – the best, the bee's knees

L

Laddie – boy
Laldy, to give it – do something enthusiastically such as singing
Laldy, to give someone – to give someone a good telling off
Lamp – hit someone or throw something
Lassie – girl, daughter, female family member
Len, take a – borrow; to take a len of a person is to exploit them
Links – bangers, sausages that are strung together

Loaded – a bad cold in the head, full of the cold

Look at the colour of – look how dirty that is

Lose the rag – lose your temper

Loupin' – jumping, painful, throbbing

Lug – ear

Lum – chimney

Lumber, to get a – to pick up someone with whom you might start a relationship

M

Ma – my, mother

Mair – more

Maist – most

Malky – to slash someone or head-butt them

Mammy – mummy

Manky – dirty, filthy

Masel' – myself

Maw – mum, mother

Meat – food, not only animal products

Merrit – married

Message bag – shopping bag

Messages, away fur the – shopping for groceries

Mibby – maybe, perhaps

Mind – remember, also used at the end of a sentence for affirmation

Minder – small gift

Mingin' – very dirty and smelly, drunk, something that was disappointing

Minted – excellent, wealthy

Miraculous – drunk

Missed yerself – you missed out by not coming to or doing something

Moan – come on

Mollocate – to thrash, beat up

Mooth – mouth

Mortalld – drunk

N

Nae – none, no

Naebody – nobody, anybody

Naeborra – no bother, no problem

Nae mair – no more

Nane – none

Naw – no

Neb – nose

Neeps – orange-fleshed turnips

Nick – to go, as in 'I'll just nick out for a minute'; prison; steal; condition, as in 'good nick'

Nip – go, borrow money

Nip a fag – pinch the end of a cigarette to put it out

No – not
Noo – now
No real – outrageous, insane
Nowt – nothing
Numpty – idiot

O

O' – of
Oan – on, own
Offy – awful
Oor – our
Oose – fluff
Oot – out
Oot scoot – out of the way
Ootside – outside
Ootsiders – the end slices of a loaf of bread
Orrabest – all the best, good luck
Ower – over
Oxter – armpit

P

Paralytic – drunk
Patter – talk, chat
Paw – father, dad

Pamp, to – to toot the horn of a car

Paralytic – very drunk

Pictures – cinema

Piece – sandwich

Pinkie – small finger

Pinnie – apron

Pit – put

Pixie – a child's woolly hat with a point

Plank – to hide; or the place where something is hidden

Playpiece – a snack that children take to school
to eat at break-time

Plook – a spot or pimple on the face

Poke – a small bag usually made of paper

Pokey hat – ice cream cone

Polis – police

Pouring – raining

Provvy cheque – a cheque from Provident Personal
Credit Ltd.

Pulley – an indoor clothes airer/dryer with wooden rails
which is attached to the ceiling and can be lowered and
raised using pulleys

Pun – pound in weight

Q

Queued out – very busy, crowded

R

Rammie – disturbance, fight

Ramorra – tomorrow

Randan, on the – out on the town, having a wild time

Rerr – very good, excellent

Rerr terr – good time

Rhyme off – recite a list or times tables

Rid raw – red raw with the cold etc.

Rigoot – outfit

Rinoo – right now

Road, in the – in the way

Rooked – skint, no money

Room 'n' kitchen – two rooms, one with a cooker and sink and another that could be used as a bedroom but often was used as the living room; the bed was in a recess in the kitchen. It may have a bathroom, or the toilet could be on the landing and shared with other tenants.

Roon, roond – round

Ruggin' – tugging, pulling

Run aboot daft or Run aboot stupid – to be very busy and in a great hurry to get things done

Runnie – take a run up to something

S

Sannie – sandwich

Sannies – sandshoes, trainers

Saunter – slow walk taking your time

Scheme – housing estate

Scratcher – bed

Screwtap – a bottle with a screw top

Scunnered, skunnered – fed up with, taken a dislike to

See if – what will happen if…

Selt – sold

Shooders – shoulders

Shoogly – loose and shaky as in a shoogly tooth

Shoot the craw – leave in a hurry, maybe in the other direction

Shot – a turn, used by children as in
 'Gee us a shot a yer bike?'

Shove – push

Shute – children's slide

Simmit – vest

Single – one

Single End – a one-room tenement flat

Skelf – splinter

Skelp – smack, hit with the hand

Skint – having no money; broke

Skirlin' – making a loud wailing noise like bagpipes

Skite – slip

Skitter – small amount, smidgen

Skiver – a shirker, someone who avoids doing their share of the work

Skoosh – fizzy drink

Sky it – run for it, make a quick exit

Slaughtered – drunk

Snib – lock on the door, especially a Yale lock where leaving the snib up or down means leaving the door unlocked or locked

Snib, The – prison

Snibbed – confined to the house by parents, grounded

Society Man – collector from the Co-operative Insurance Society

So it does – yes it does, used as confirmation at the end of a sentence.

Sook – suck

Sore hand – a runny jam sandwich in white bread as it looks like a bandage with dripping blood

Spanner – can-opener

Spelder'd – spread out

Spent – worn out

Squinty – not straight, on a slant

Stairheid – the landing in a tenement

Stank – drain in the street

Stankie – game of marbles using holes in a stank

Steamie – wash-house

Steamin' – drunk

Stinker – a dirty look

Stinkin' rotten – horrible

Stoat – bounce

Stoater – something or someone that is really good, fantastic

Stoatin' doon – raining heavily

Stooky – a plaster cast on a broken bone; a person who stands around and does nothing

Stoorie – dusty

Stooshie – hullabaloo, big row

Stormer – excellent

Stoshus – very drunk

Stousie – stout

Stumpie – short

Subway – Glasgow Underground Railway System

Sugarollie – liquorice

Sure – yes, often used in confirmation

Swally – drink

Swatch – a quick look

Sweeties – sweets, confectionery

T

Tackety boots – strong boots with tacks to reinforce toes and heels

Tae – to

Taes – toes

Take – have when referring to illness, as in take a heart attack

Tartan paint – something a new apprentice is sent to fetch as well as a long stand

Tatties – potatoes

Telt – told

Teuchters – people from the Scottish Highlands or the Western Isles

That's a sin – that's a shame

The day – today

The Fair – Glasgow factory/shipyards holiday during the last two weeks of July

The gether – together

The Toon – Glasgow City Centre

This is me – this is what has happened to me

Thorn – nail

Thrapple – throat

Thrifty – money box

Throw a flaky – outburst of bad temper

Toaty – very small

Ton weight – very heavy

Trilin' – tapping, knocking

Tummle yer wilkies – turn a somersault

Tumshie – yellow-fleshed turnip, stupid person

U

Up in the air – a plan that has had to be cancelled or now uncertain

Up the Toon, to go – to go to Glasgow City Centre

Ur – are

Urnae – aren't

V

Vickie Road – Victoria Road

Vickie, The – Royal Victoria Hospital

W

Wa' – wall

Wabbit – exhausted, worn out

Wae – with

Wallies – false teeth

Wally close – the entrance to a tenement which has tiled walls

Wan – one

Wance – once

Wanner – to do something with only one attempt

Wasnae – was not

Waste – to spoil a thing or a child

Watter – water

Waukrife – unable to sleep, wakeful

Wean – child

Wee – small, young, also used to stress friendliness of a situation – *'Will ye no hiv a wee cuppa tea?'* Neither the cup nor the amount of tea will be smaller than usual.

Wee soul – a term of affection or pity for someone

Well-fired – well-done toast or streak etc.

What are you fur? – What would you like?
The reply is *'I'm fur a pokey hat.'*

Wheesht – be quiet

Whit – what

Whitever – whatever

Wi' – with

Wid – would

Winchin' – snogging, kissing

Windae – window

Wirsels – ourselves

Wisnae – wasn't

Worky up – used by children to describe a method of making a playground swing start moving and then

working it up to a good height on their own without the
swing being pushed by an adult

Wullnae – won't

Wumman – woman

Wur – our, were

X, Y, Z

Ya, Yah, Ye – you

Ya beauty – that's great

Ya dancer – great, really good

Ye are so – 'Yes you are', usually used in a dispute
or for emphasis

Yer – your

Yer not on – no chance

Yin – one

Yir – your

Yon – those, them, that

Youse – plural of you

Wee Willie Winkie
by **William Miller** *(1810–1872)* who was born in Glasgow and described on his gravestone in the Necropolis as 'The Laureate of the Nursery'

William Miller –
Laureate of the Nursery

Wee Willie Winkie, rins through the toun,
Up stairs and doon stairs, in his nicht-gown,
Tirling at the windaes, crying at the lock,
'Are the weans in their bed, fur it's noo ten o'clock?'

Hey, Willie Winkie, are you coming ben,
The cat's singing grey thrums to the sleeping hen,
The dog's speldert on the floor and disna gie a cheep
But here's a waukrife laddie that winna fa' asleep.

Onything but sleep, you rogue, glow'rin' like the moon,
Rattling in an airn jug, wi 'an airn spoon,
Rumblin' tumblin', roon aboot, crawing like a cock,
Skirlin' like a kenna-what, wauk'nin' sleeping folk.

Hey Willie Winkie – The wean's in a creel
Wamblin' aff a bodie's knee, like a very eel,
Ruggin' at the cat's lug, ravelin' a' her thrums,
Hey Willie Winkie – See, there he comes!

Wearied is the mither, that has a stoorie wean,
A wee stumpie, stousie, that canna rin his lane.
That has a battle aye wi' sleep, afore he'll close an e'e –
But a kiss frae aff his rosy lips, gies strength anew to me.

Crossing the road in Govan.
The British Linen Bank is on the corner

Dae ye know hen, even efter fifty years Ah can remember those
school jotters wi 'A moment at the kerb is better than a month in
hospital'. Mind you, Ah canny think whit Ah wrote in them.

Food

Family gathered around the range in the kitchen

Porridge is traditionally made with handfuls of oatmeal stirred into boiling water and then cooked slowly. When ready, it is served hot, with cold milk poured around the edge of the bowl, and probably covered in salt. Leftover porridge would be put aside to set and the cold porridge cut into slices or caulders and eaten cold or fried with eggs, fish or bacon.

Lorne sausage comes in two varieties, square-sliced or round-sliced. The slices are cut off at the request of the customer. It is a bit like a meat loaf and not at all like bangers, which are called links. A piece or roll and sausage would be made with Lorne sausage and not links. It was the

Glasgow comedian **Tommy Lorne** *(1890–1935)* who made so many jokes about square-sliced during his Music Hall acts that his name was given to this type of sausage.

Tattie scones are made from leftover mashed potatoes, butter and flour. This mixture is rolled out into a round and marked into quarters and then cooked on a hot griddle or flat pan for a few minutes until both sides have a dark-brown mottled surface.

The Glasgow Roll is a morning roll with a hard outside and a soft chewy inside – great with hot fillings such as bacon and eggs. McGee's Bakery produces 26 million of these rolls every year as well as tattie scones, Scotch pancakes, Empire biscuits and tea bread including white snowballs and yum-yums. Yum-yums are a bit like long doughnuts, with a twist in the middle, and Empire biscuits are really two biscuits sandwiched together with jam and topped with icing and a red glacé cherry. The McGee family have been baking in Glasgow since 1935 and their first bakehouse was in Oran Street in Maryhill. From here they moved to Murano Street and they are now in the M8 Food Park where they bake over two million bread rolls, of many varieties, every day. If you go to the fitba' you may well find McGee's Scotch pies on sale, including their lower fat version 'Wi'oot the greese'.

Cock-a-leekie soup is a warming winter soup made from leeks, potatoes and chicken stock.

Cullen skink is a soup made from smoked haddock, milk, onions and potatoes, seasoned with parsley and black pepper.

Mince and Tatties are not served like a cottage pie with the potatoes on the top but with the mince and mashed tatties placed separately on the plate. Carrots and onions are cooked with the mince and sometimes neeps are boiled with the tatties and they are bashed together. Dumplings are also a popular addition as this makes the meat go further.

> *Ma grannie wid ask the butcher for a pun a best stewing steak and when he had done that she wid ask him to mince it so that she knew exactly what was in her mince!*

Haggis with bashed neeps and tatties is the traditional Burn's Supper served on 25th January to celebrate Scotland's national poet **Rabbie Burns** *(1759–1796)*. Haggis is made from a mixture of sheep or lamb's lights, hearts and liver mixed with oatmeal, onions, suet and seasoning and boiled in a bung made from the intestines of a sheep or lamb.

Bridies are shaped like Cornish pasties but the pastry is flaky and they contain meat, suet and onions.

Clootie dumpling is a pudding boiled in a cloth; and on special occasions, as well as the ingredients, there would be silver thruppenny bits, wrapped in greaseproof paper and hidden in the mixture. This dumpling is not as rich as a Christmas pudding. The ingredients include suet, flour, breadcrumbs, oatmeal, dried fruit, eggs, buttermilk or fresh milk soured with lemon juice, grated cooking apple, cinnamon, ginger and nutmeg.

Cranachan makes a delicious dessert but it can also be served for breakfast. It is made from crunchy oat cereal, thick yogurt and Scottish raspberries. For a less healthy version use thickly whipped cream instead of yogurt.

Cream cookies are round, sweet buns with shiny brown tops which are split and filled with whipped cream and dusted with icing sugar.

Fish supper: If you are off to the Chippie here are a few new words that could be useful. If you only want one fish that's a single fish and a bag of chips is a poke of chips. Fish and chips are called a fish supper, haggis and chips a haggis supper and pizza and chips a pizza supper so I expect you are getting the hang of this now. Lavish amounts of salt and vinegar will be offered along with red and brown sauce. Other options include black pudding, fritters and deep-fried Mars Bars.

Barr's IRN-BRU: Wash down your supper with a can of IRN-BRU, first made in 1901 and advertised as 'Your other national drink – made in Scotland from girders'. It was originally called 'Iron Brew' and Adam Brown, the famous Highland athlete from Shotts, was shown on the label. New food labelling regulations insisting that brand names should be literally true forced the company to re-brand. Although the drink did contain iron, it was not brewed and the new trade mark, IRN-BRU, was registered in July 1946. Barr's introduced the returnable glass bottle in 1905 and a halfpenny was paid to customers for every bottle returned to the shop.

The secret recipe for IRN-BRU contains thirty-two ingredients and is passed down from generation to generation. Robert F. Barr set up his soft drinks business in 1887 on the Great Eastern Road in Glasgow and nowadays IRN-BRU is produced, warehoused and distributed from Cumbernauld where 690 million cans are produced each year; and in Scotland over 700 cans are sold every minute!

Tunnock's teacakes: Thomas Tunnock's first bakery was opened in Uddingston in 1890 and their present business is still nearby. These teacakes have a round biscuit base topped with a scoop of marshmallow and are covered in chocolate.

Corolla Ice Cream Van

An Oyster and a Pokey Hat

The ice cream van would come round the scheme and you'd hear the chimes first. Then we wid be asking my maw 'Hiv ye ony ginger bottles?' In those days you got a penny back on the glass bottles and this would go towards the price of a pokey hat.

Pokey hat – cone filled with ice cream. This may come from the early Italian Ice Cream sellers shouting *'Gelati, ecco un poco!'* ('Here's a little ice cream').

McCallum – ice cream with a raspberry sauce

Double nougat (pronounced 'nugget') – wafer filled with mock cream and coated with chocolate; ice cream is sandwiched between two of these.

Single nougat – ice cream sandwiched between a nougat and a wafer

Oyster – two oyster-shaped wafers filled with ice cream. One of them has some marshmallow in it and is partly covered with chocolate and sprinkled with coconut.

Ma brother's cat would go out and join the queue along wi aw the weans at the ice cream van and he wis such a character that the ice cream man would throw him doon the end of a pokey hat with a wee drop of ice cream.

Coulter's Candy

Robert Coulter made aniseed-flavoured toffee and sold it at markets and fairs in the late 1800s. His advertising technique was to play a whistle and sing a song promoting his candy. Here's my grannie's version.

Here comes Coulter doon the street
The man the weans aw like tae meet.
His big black bag does haud a treat
'Cos its foo o' Coulter's Candy.

Ally, bally, ally bally bee,
Sittin' on yer mammy's knee
Greetin' for a wee bawbee,
Tae buy mair Coulter's Candy.

Mammy gie me ma thrifty doon,
Here's auld Coulter comin' roon'
Wi' a basket on his croon,
Sellin' Coulter's Candy.

Poor wee Annie's greetin' tae,
Sae whit can puir Mammy dae,
But gie them a penny atween them twae,
Tae buy mair Coulter's Candy.

Poor wee Jeanie's lookin' affa thin,
A rickle o' banes covered wi' skin,
Noo she's getting' a wee double chin,
Wi' sookin' Coulter's Candy.

Glesga made the Clyde and the Clyde made Glesga

Albert Bridge in the 1890s
Shutterstock ©Morphart Creation

The Clyde Trust's new 175 ton crane at Finnieston Quay, Glasgow
where it is being tested to a load of 200 tons, 1932

The Clyde starts its journey to the sea in the Lanarkshire hills, seventy miles from Glasgow, flows quickly at the Falls of Clyde and steadies down to flow through Glasgow, perhaps reluctant to leave a place where it is well loved. The river used to be shallow at the estuary and the deepwater ports were at Dumbarton and Irvine. During the 18th and 19th centuries, engineers deepened the Clyde and built docks right up to the city centre. Merchant ships from around the world then sailed up the Clyde to Glasgow and larger ships were built here. As the tonnage of the ships increased, sections of the Clyde were too shallow for them and in 1852 a steamer on the Glasgow to New York route grounded on rocks at Elderslie. At first they thought it was just a big boulder but it turned out to be a bed of whinstone, 900 feet (275m) long and 300 feet (90m) wide. The obstacle was blasted with gunpowder but in the end a new powerful explosive called dynamite had to be used.

By the early 1900s, Glasgow was known as the 'Second City of the Empire'. An amazing 30 per cent of all the ships in the world were Clydebuilt. Robert Gillespie wrote in 1876 '... *the workmanship is so superior that "Clydebuilt" has everywhere become a warrant for excellence. Vessels of all sizes and classes are turned out from the river yards. Iron-clad frigates such as the Black Prince, heavily plated rams such as the Hotspur, troop-ships such as the Malabar, have left the Clyde...*' (Glasgow and the Clyde, 1876)

Wi' a' oor fauts, by Goad, we ken jist hoo to lay a keel,
An' build a boat that nane can beat in a' the warld beside,
The best o' wark, the bonniest boats aye come frae oot the Clyde.

(**B. Kennedy**, Victorian poet)

Launch of the 18,500-ton Ruahine at John Brown's Yard,
Clydebank, December 1950

The shipyards, bonded warehouses, granaries and all
the associated trades employed thousands. Iron and coal
were readily available and railways and canals made
transporting them cheap and easy. The settlements along
the river expanded and eventually they merged into a
sprawling Glasgow. Govan has been around since AD 600
and only became incorporated into Glasgow in 1912. Ships
are still built there by BAE Systems at Fairfields Yards,

whose origins date back to the 1870s. Other well-known ship builders were Elders, Stephens, Yarrows, Lithgows and John Brown's of Clydebank.

The Queens of the Clyde

The British Queen was built by John Wood of Port Glasgow and was, in the 1830s, the largest steamer afloat. Her engines were 40 horsepower which was, at that time, considered an extraordinary size.

The Fire Queen, launched in 1845, was the first iron-built streamer with a screw propeller built at Glasgow. She was 135 tons and fitted with double engines with a total of 80 horse power.

John Brown's shipyard at Clydebank built war ships and three 'Queen' liners for Cunard. In 1914, over 10,000 workers were employed here.

The Queen Mary was built at John Brown's and launched in September 1934. The shipping line's brochure described her in glowing terms. 'In each class a degree of spaciousness, comfort and refinement has been attained which has never previously been attempted on so large a scale.' During the Second World War, the Queen Mary served as a troopship, nicknamed 'Grey Ghost' as she was repainted battleship grey. She is now a hotel and tourist attraction in Long Beach, California.

The Queen Elizabeth was also built at John Brown's and when she was launched on 27 September 1938 the Daily Record and Mail reported that invited guests would be expected to wear cut-away coats, silk hats and Garden Party finery. The Queen Elizabeth was thought to be vital to the war effort so she was painted battleship grey and converted to a troopship. It was only after the war that she took up her role as a luxury passenger liner. She retired in 1968 and it was thought that she would be refitted as a hotel in southern Florida but this did not work out. A Chinese businessman, who planned to turn her into a floating University, bought her but before the refit was completed several blazes broke out on the ship and she capsized and sank in Hong Kong Harbour. Most of her hull is now buried under the runway at Hong Kong's airport.

The Queen Elizabeth II (QEII), the last great passenger liner to be built on the Clyde, came from John Brown's yard and a quarter of a million people witnessed her launch on 20 September 1967. She served as a troopship in the Falklands War and retired from service in 2008. Her future still hangs in the balance.

The Influence of Venice

The Old
Templeton's
Carpet Factory

No many people wid think of designing their factory in the
style of a Venetian palace but **James Templeton** *(1802–1883)*
wis fair scunnered wi the council's objections tae his plans
tae build a new factory on a very desirable site overlooking
Glasgow Green so he commissioned the Scottish architect
William Leiper *(1839–1916)* to design his new carpet
factory in the 'Palladian Gothic' style, reminiscent of the
Doge's Palace in Venice. Templeton's Carpet Factory, with
its circular windows, turrets, arches and orange, yellow and
blue bricks, is certainly an eye-catching building. However,
the construction was not without tragedy as a new wall
collapsed during high winds on 1 November 1889, trapping
100 women workers and killing twenty-nine women and
girls in the weaving sheds. Templeton's famous, richly

coloured, chenille Axminster carpets graced grand houses and ocean liners, including the Titanic.

The People's Palace and Fountain

Along the road from Templeton's is the People's Palace Museum with its large steel-framed Winter Gardens. It was designed by city engineer **A. B. McDonald** and constructed in red sandstone. The East End of Glasgow was a poor, unhealthy and overcrowded area in 1898 when the Peoples' Palace opened, offering opportunities for self-improvement with reading rooms, an art gallery and a museum, open to all. You can still visit it today and discover the history of Glaswegians from the 18th century to the present day. It is a friendly museum with helpful staff. In front of the museum is the Doulton Fountain, the largest terracotta fountain in the world.

The influence of Venice can also be seen in **John Honeyman's** *(1831–1914)* design for Ca' d'Oro, a carpet and furniture warehouse built in 1872, on the corner of Union Street and Gordon Street. Based on the Venetian Ca' d'Oro, a palace on the Grand Canal, the building has arches above the shops, and large bay windows framed by Doric and Corinthian columns with round windows above. In the 1920s an extra floor was added to what was then the Ca' d'Oro Tea Rooms and Grill. Downstairs in the gentlemen's smoking room was a view of Venice by J. W. Ferguson and on the first floor was the Venetian Tea Room. Unfortunately, the interior of the building was gutted by fire in the 1980s but the exterior was restored in the 1990s.

Ca' d'Oro, Glasgow

The Gates to the Bridge of Sighs and the Necropolis

David Hamilton *(1768–1843)* and his son **James** *(1818–1861)* designed the Cemetery Lodge, the Superintendent's House, the Egyptian Vaults, the Bridge of Sighs and the gates to the Necropolis in Glasgow.

The Bridge of Sighs was built across the Molendinar Burn to link the Cathedral to the new Necropolis and is a reference to the Ponte dei Sospiri in Venice which linked the criminal courts with the city's prison. However, Glasgow's Bridge of Sighs looks nothing like the bridge in Venice and its name probably has more to do with the sighing of the mourners crossing from the Cathedral to the Necropolis.

Crazy aboot the game

Here are a couple of verses of a traditional Scottish song about fitba' that was probably written in the 1880s by James Curran. Perhaps not much has changed. There are modern versions of this song made famous by Robin Hall and Jimmy McGregor about a fitba' crazy Jock McGraw.

You aa know ma big brither Jock, his right name's Jonny Shaw,
He's lately jined a fitba' club, for he's mad aboot fitba'.
He has two black eyes already and teeth oot by the root,
Since Jock's face came in contact wi another fella's boot.

Chorus:
'Cos he's fitba' crazy, he's fitba' mad,
The fitba' it has ta'en away the wee bit sense he had,
And it wid take a dozen servants, his claes tae wash and scrub,
Since Jock became a member o' that terrible fitba' club.

His wife she says she'll leave him, if Jock he doesnae keep
Away frae playing fitba' at night time in his sleep.
He ca's her Pat McGinty an' ither names sae droll,
Last night he kicked her oot of bed an' swore it was a goal!

Chorus :
'Cos he's fitba' crazy…

Doon the Watter

Enjoying a day out at Troon, 1954

Saltcoats, 1953

A Clyde Steamer leaving the Broomielaw for a sail 'doon the watter' in the early 1950s

The Glasgow Fair began as a market where merchants from outside the city could trade and it ran for a week from 7 July as this was the day the Cathedral was dedicated in 1136. If this date fell on a Sunday, the Fair could not begin until the Monday. Eventually it was decided that the Glasgow Fair would begin on the third Monday in July. In 1810, the Fair moved from Stockwell Street to Glasgow Green and become more of an entertainment with sideshows, hobby-horses and drinking booths.

The Fair Fortnight is when the shipyards and factories closed for their summer holidays. It wis braw tae go tae the seaside wi yir bucket and spade. St Enoch's Station wis dead busy wi trains tae the Ayrshire coast like Saltcoats and Troon. Doon the watter, on the Firth of Clyde, wir the seaside resorts of Dunoon and Rothsay. Sometimes maw, paw and the weans wid go for a week or a fortnight but there wis also day trips doon the watter and families queued at the Broomielaw fur the steamer. When ye wir skint yir holiday destination wis hameldaeme.

There was also a darker side to **Glasgow Green** as sixty-seven men and women were executed by hanging there between 1814 and 1865. Over 200 crimes carried the death penalty in those days. The last person to be hanged at Glasgow Green was Dr Prichard and 80,000 people turned up to watch.

From 1865 until 1928, hangings took place at Duke Street Prison at 8am. A black flag was raised and a bell tolled when the executed prisoner was declared dead. Hangings then took place at Barlinnie Prison until they were abolished.

Gie it laldy! C'moan belt it oot!

Great for a sing-along on a bus trip as it can go on and on by adding more and more relatives…

Oh ye cannae shove yer grannie affa bus,
Oh ye cannae shove yer grannie affa bus,
Ye cannae shove yer grannie,
For she's yer mammy's mammy,
Ye cannae shove yer grannie affa bus.

Ye can shove yer other grannie affa bus,
Ye can shove yer other grannie affa bus,
Ye can shove yer other grannie,
Fur she's yer daddy's mammy,
Ye can shove yer other grannie affa bus.

Oot an' Aboot

A bottle a skoosh: No, it is not alcohol or drugs, it is another name for ginger – a bottle of fizzy drink. Probably called this as it goes skoosh when you open the top!

Ah'll malkie ye: This is not a good thing to hear as it means much the same as a Glasgow kiss or 'Ah'll stick the heid on ye'. The next thing you are likely to remember is waking up in hospital.

St Enoch's Church and St Enoch's Subway Station with 'Trains for Hillhead, Partick, Ibrox, Govan every 3 minutes' emblazoned on the roof

Ah wish ye the health tae wear it: This is a nice thing to say when someone shows you their new rigoot.

Carry oot: Alcohol bought from an off-licence shop or supermarket. If you are going to a party in Glasgow you will be expected take a carry oot.

C'moan get aff: This is your bus stop. Get off now. You have arrived at your destination.

Ferranuff: This constitutes an agreement of sorts and is used quite a lot in conversation. It means fair enough or OK.

Haud yer wheesht: Everyone likes a good blether in Glasgow so ye must be talking during the big picture, taking rubbish or not listening to the other person. Just be quite.

High Tea: This is a lot more than a cup of tea and is eaten late in the afternoon or early evening. It is a small meal, maybe poached egg on toast or even fish and chips, served with a pot of tea.

When ah went tae the seaside wi ma grannie fur the day we wid go and hiv a High Tea afore wi came hame on the train. This wis a special treat as we hid a High Tea instead of something tae eat at dinnertime.

Kelvinside Accent: You will know if you hear someone from Kelvinside in a posh shop. The words are the same but the pronunciation is exaggerated and of a higher pitch. There is a tendency to pronounce the letter a as a long e, as in 'Fancy that!' which becomes 'Feencee thet!' In a tearoom look out for pinkies sticking out when they are holding their teacups – a wee giveaway that they might be from Kelvinside!

Knock-back: If you turn up tae a casino or a posh nightclub wearing the wrang gear such as jeans and a simmit you'll be guaranteed a knock-back – they'll no' let ye in.

The Subway: This is not a sandwich but the Underground Transport System with its own distinctive smell and noisy trains. It is the only completely underground system in Britain as the others, like the London Tube and Newcastle's

Metro, have sections where the trains travel above ground. The Subway, which opened on 14 December 1896, is the third oldest underground in the world after London and Budapest. The stations have central platforms so the trains are always boarded from their right-hand side and there are therefore no doors on the left. As none of the passengers saw the left sides of the trains, they never bothered to paint them. Cable traction was used to operate the system until 1935 when it was converted to electricity.

Dae ye think it'ill rain the day, hen?

Whit the weather 'ill dae the day is a great wee topic of conversation in the Toon. Ah wis on a bus the other day – it wis a Saturday – and there wis a load o' tourists who wir drookit, drippin' wet an' a wee bit subdued. The rain wis lashing doon and ye couldnae see oot the windaes as they wir aw steamed up on the inside. A man said to them 'Aw, terrible weather the day? Last year we hid a great summer.' The tourists were now wishing they'd came tae Glesga last year, when he continued 'Ah remember it well – it wis on a Tuesday. Mind you it didnae last aw day!'

George Square in the snow

You'll no be surprised that Glesga is jist aboot the same latitude as Moscow an' the winds in the winter wid freeze a brass monkey. Ah wis brought up in Glesga in the days afore central heating when the ice wis on the inside o' the windaes and there wis nae running hot watter – ye hid tae boil a kettle or a big pot if ye wur gonna dae mair than gee yur face a lick an' a promise. We weans wore liberty bodices during the winter – lucky if ye had two as one could be put in the wash, otherwise ye'd wear the same wan aw winter! Mostly we wore wellies and splashed through puddles and made slides in the snow on oor way to school in Govan. It wis a lang walk but we didnae hiv a car or even a bike. The radiators in the school were biling hot and we had a nice teacher who let us put oor mits and woolly hats there to dry. It wis a bit of a nuisance if yir granny had sewn yir mitts on a lang bit o' lastic so yid no loose them. Yid just be getting warm – Ah loved school in the winter as it wis the ony place that wis warm – when the wee bottles o' milk would be brought to the classroom by the Jannie. Sometimes when we took the top off, the milk would still be icy and it wis hard to get the straw in. When Ah wis wee Ah mind the summers being sunny, warm an' long. We played outside maist o' the time and when it rained, we'd just played up a close. If ye were hungry you'd shout up tae yir Ma to throw ye doon a jeely piece – best if it wis an ender.

The Merchant City

The Tobacco Lords

In the 18th century it was much quicker – twenty days quicker – to travel from Glasgow to Virginia in America than to do the same journey from London. As a result, Glasgow became one of the most popular ports for the tobacco trade. Importing tobacco was big business and was controlled by a an elite group of Tobacco Lords or Virginian Dons who dressed in red cloaks, carried gold-topped canes and proudly paraded on the plainstanes in front of the Tolbooth at Glasgow Cross. **John Glassford of Douglaston** *(1715–1783)* was one of them and his townhouse at Trongate, Shawfield Mansion, even had a deer park. The Tobacco Lords did not pay cash for their tobacco leaves but exchanged them for all manner of goods, such as Delftfield Pottery, and this helped to increase their profit margins. Many Tobacco Lords had streets named after them, including Andrew Buchanan, James Dunlop and Archibald Ingram. After the American War of Independence tobacco was no longer Glasgow's most lucrative trade. The demand for textiles increased and there were many spinning factories before the days of steam power. At the South Woodside Cotton Mill at Kelvinbridge (built in 1784 and demolished in 1894) the spinners were dependent on the flow of the River Kelvin. When it was in full flow the workers had to work all hours but when the river was low there was no work at all.

The Barras

The Barrowland Ballrooom

Rag and Bone Man

Hawkers sold clothes, fish, fruit, crockery and all sorts of things from barrows throughout Glasgow. Some had pitches, like the flower seller outside Lewis's, and others travelled around, perhaps with a pony and cart, shouting 'Coal briquetts' or 'Any ol' rags'. If the weans handed over a few rags they got a balloon in exchange, and Maw might get a bit of crockery for a bag full. Rags could also be bought from Ritchie's Rag Store in Stevenson Street, and these would be taken to the steamie and washed, ready to sell on at a higher price from their barras. The Barras was a market where many of the hawkers would gather on a Saturday. **Maggie McIver** *(1879–1958)* was 'Queen o' the Barras' as she developed an enterprising business hiring out her 300 barras from her yard at Marshall Lane. As it rains quite a lot in Glasgow, she came up with the idea of building an enclosed market in Moncur Street. Every Christmas Maggie gave all the hawkers a free meal, a dance and a drink. In 1934 she was unable to book her usual hall so she built her own Barrowland Ballroom and it opened just in time on Christmas Eve. By 1948, the dance floor in the Barrowland Ballroom held 2,000 dancers. It was a very popular venue and the queues would line the Gallowgate, Gibson Street and Moncur Street on a Friday night.

The Barras was full of characters and it was an entertainment to go there even if you were not looking to buy. Prince Monululu, the tipster who dressed in an exotic style, would offer tips straight from the horse's mouth. Lascar seamen would buy hats and pile them on their heads, one on top of the other. They drove a hard bargain and paid very little for their purchases. Some people made their own products such as feet wash, made from water, whitening and Eau-de-Cologne from Woolworth's. This was a popular remedy for sore feet but it may be that just washing them made them feel better, especially as many feet were not washed for months on end! There was perfume that lasted for days and days as it was made from watered-down floral disinfectant. The patter was always good and one hawker used to offer a cigarette lighter and a coat hanger for 1d. When the customer opened the packet, it contained a match and a nail!

Noo hen, if ye huvtae borra money, borra it fae one o' those pessimists, 'cos they'll no expect it back!

Ah hear wee Duggie's deed – **whit happened tae him?**
Och, he got scared hauf tae death – **twice!**

Glasgow Botanic Gardens

Glasgow Botanic Gardens were founded in 1817 by **Thomas Hopkirk** *(1785–1841)*, a botanist who donated his own plant collection to the first site at Sandyford. The collection grew to such an extent that the gardens moved to their present site on the banks of the River Kelvin in 1842. Professor **William Jackson Hooker** *(1785–1865)*, the Regius Chair of Botany at Glasgow University, guided the development of the gardens from 1821 until he was appointed Director of the Royal Botanic Gardens at Kew in 1841.

Entrance to the Botanic Gardens, The Gates
at Great Western Road, 1923

The Victorian entrepreneur **John Kibble** *(1815–1894)* built a huge glasshouse at his home in Coulport, Loch Long. This Kibble Crystal Art Palace was designed by Boucher and Cousland and built by James Boyd & Sons of Paisley. In 1871, Kibble offered his Palace to the Botanic Gardens and the structure was dismantled and towed on rafts down Loch Long and up the Clyde and then along the River Kelvin. When it was re-erected Kibble extended the transepts at his own expense and added the large circular dome, some 150 feet in diameter. The deal was that he could hold 'entertainments' there, charging an entry fee, for twenty years and then he would donate the building to the Botanic Gardens. It must have been a marvellous sight when it opened in 1873, lit by six hundred gas jets.

Fàilte gu Glaschu

As well as the Glasgow Dialect you may come across some Gaelic so here are a few useful words and phrases.

Glasgow Central Railway Station – **Glaschu Mheadhain**

Goodbye – **Mar sin leibh/leat**

Good Health/Cheers! – **Slàinte mhath!** and the reply is: Great health to you everyday that I see you and every day that I don't – **Slàinte mhor a h-uile là a chi 's nach fhaic**

Good morning – **Madainn mhath**

Good night – **Oidhche mhath**

Happy Birthday – **Là breith sona dhuit/dhuibh**
How are you? – **Ciamar a tha thu/sibh?** (**Thu** = you
singular and friends; **sibh** = you plural and is more formal)
Queen Street Railway Station – **Sràid na Banrighinn**
Thank you – **Taing mhór**
Welcome to Glasgow – **Fàilte gu Glaschu**
Welcome to Scotland! – **Fàilte gu Alba!**
Whisky – **uisge-beatha**
Wine – **fion**

'Rear'd amang the
heather, you can
see he's Scottish
built, By the wig,
wig, wiggle, wiggle,
waggle o' the kilt.'
from 'The Waggle
o' the Kilt' by
Sir Harry Lauder

COUNTING IN GAELIC

One – **aon**	Five – **còig**	Nine – **naoi**
Two – **dà**	Six – **sia**	Ten – **deich**
Three – **trì**	Seven – **seachd**	
Four – **ceithir**	Eight – **ochd**	

The Glasgow School of Art

Charles Rennie Mackintosh *(1868–1928)* was born at 70 Parson Street in Glasgow. He was a student at the Glasgow School of Art from 1883 to 1894 and from 1889 worked as a draughtsman with the architectural firm Honeyman and Keppie. They won the competition to design a new Glasgow School of Art with one of Mackintosh's designs. Today the students at the School of Art give interesting and enthusiastic tours of their building, which has been a working art school for more than a century. They also offer Glasgow Style City Walking Tours and details can be found on their website: **www.gsa.ac.uk.**

Glasgow School of Art

The Willow Tea Rooms

Don't tell me ye've finished that 100-piece jigsaw at last,
Paw? Hoo lang his that taken ye?
Ony aboot six months.
Dae ye no think that's a lang time?
Och, no – it says three to five years on the box!

The Burrell Collection

William Burrell *(1861–1958)* was born into a shipping family
and on his father's death in 1875 he took over running the firm
with his brother. They made the best of every opportunity by
ordering new ships when the market was in a slump and selling
them at a large profit when the market recovered. William
married Constant Mitchell, the daughter of a shipping family,

in 1901. During the First World War, the Burrell Brothers sold most of their fleet and made so much money that William effectively retired and became an art collector. He had a good eye for a bargain and enjoyed haggling with dealers, but he was a traditionalist and did not collect a great deal of modern art and so there are few paintings later than Degas or sculptures later than Rodin in his collection, with the exception of Cézanne and Epstein. Burrell was an avid collector of Chinese ceramics, tapestries, stained glass, silver, bronzes, Indian and Persian rugs, furniture and architectural features. In 1944 he gave most of his collection to the City of Glasgow along with a generous donation to construct a building to house it. It was not until the 1970s that a specially designed building was constructed in the grounds of the Pollock Country Park to display his collection. This is an extraordinary and stunning space with items from the collection being incorporated into the fabric of the building.

When Ah went tae the Burrell jist efter it opened, it wis the most modern museum Ah 'ad ever seen. There were nae dark dusty corners and everything wis bright and airy. Ah had to go again and again as there wis so much natural light, the exhibits looked different as the seasons changed. Ah wis amazed at the stain glass windaes, huge doors and stone arches that were incorporated into the building and could be walked through or looked through. Over forty years later, Ah still enjoy visiting the Burrell.

Dusting the
Burrell Collection

The Clydebank Blitz

During the Second World War there were hundreds of air-raid shelters all over the city in tenement basements, tunnels and under railway arches. Eighty-three large electric sirens were set up across the city to warn everyone when to take shelter. The Kelvin Hall became a mortuary with space for up to 700 bodies and Air Raid Wardens checked the city to make sure no lights could be seen during the blackout. The first air raid on Glasgow took place in July 1940 and the worst bombings were on 13 and 14 March 1941.

Bomb damage

Evacuees with their luggage and gas masks

Women delivering
coal in wartime
Shutterstock
©IgorGolovniov

The munitions factories and shipyards along the River Clyde were attacked by 260 bombers on the first night. Waves of incendiary bombs, land-mines and high-explosive bombs were dropped over a period of nine hours. When people emerged from the shelters, fires were raging, the streets were devastated and many people were trapped in buildings that had collapsed. The next night 200 bombers returned and the raids continued for nearly eight hours. During these two nights 528 civilians died and over 48,000 were made homeless.

Hey bad-a-ree-bab, ma mammy's got a prefab!
Prefabs were built all over Glasgow after the war to help solve the housing shortage caused by the bombing. These homes were made from prefabricated parts and were intended to be a temporary solution but they were in use up until the 1990s.

A Guid New Year tae yin an' aw...

Military Tattoo Band Playing in Glasgow, 2010
Shutterstock ©Stefan Bogren

The thing Ah remember aboot New Year in Glasgow when Ah wis wee wis the bellowing sound of the ship's horns aw going off at midnight to welcome in the New Year. We'd open the windaes to let the Old Year oot an' the New Year in. Sometimes we could hear the sound of the ships' fog horns when we wakened up in the morning and then we knew it was foggy ootside without opening the curtains.

Auld Lang Syne is sung at New Year, at the end of a Burn's Supper and other occasions. Everyone stands in a circle and holds hands and sings until the last chorus when they rush in and out of the circle the best they can depending on how much celebrating they have been doing. Here are the first and last verses.

Auld Lang Syne by Rabbie Burns *(1759–1796)*

Should auld acquaintance be forgot,
And never brought to mind?
Should auld acquaintance be forgot,
And auld lang syne?

Chorus:
For auld lang syne, my jo,
For auld lang syne,
We'll tak a cup of kindness yet,
For auld lang syne!
And there's a hand my trusty friend,
And gie's a hand o' thine,
And we'll tak a right guid willie waught,
For auld lang syne

Chorus: For auld land syne …

Just when you think that the evening's over, everyone starts to sing:

We're No' Awa' Tae Bide Awa'

Here's the chorus and a couple of verses:

Chorus
For we're no' awa' tae bide awa',
For we're no' awa' tae le'e ye,
For we're no awa' tae bide awa',
We'll aye come back an' see ye.

As I gaed doon by Wilsontoon,
I met auld Johnnie Scobbie,
Says I to him will ye hae a hauf,
Says he 'Man! That's my hobby.'

Chorus: For we're no' awa' …

We wandered doon the street again,
We clikit unco cherry,
When John got hame his wife cried 'Shame!
I see your enjoyin' yir hobby.'

Chorus: For we're no' awa' …

Whit! Did ye no know that?

Argyle Street

Argyle Street *'is the finest part; it has a mixture of old and new buildings, but it is long enough and lofty enough to be one of the best streets in G. Britain.'* However **Robert Southey** *(1774–1843)*, the Poet Laureate, who arrived in Glasgow in 1819 accompanied by **Thomas Telford** *(1757–1834)*, the engineer, also said: *'We drove to the Buck's Head in Argyle Street. Large as this house is, they had no room with a fire, when we arrived cold and hungry, at 10 o'clock on a wet morning.'*

Babcock & Wilcox: These American engineers opened a sales office in Glasgow in 1881 and the first Babcock boiler was supplied to the Singer Manufacturing Company works in Kilbowie. Singers, best known for their sewing machines, came to Glasgow in the 1850s and opened a large factory in Bridgeton in 1871.

Harry Churchill and his son started a business making hand-built prams in 1927 and soon Churchill Prams had a reputation for excellence. The baby boom after the Second World War brought an increase in demand and Churchill's continued making prams in Tradeston until the 1980s.

James Watt came up with the idea of the separate steam engine condenser while walking on Glasgow Green. Watt himself wrote 'I had not walked further than the golf-house when the whole thing was arranged in my mind.'

Sir Thomas Lipton *(1850–1931)* of Lipton's Tea fame was born in the Gorbals and opened his first shop in Stobcross Street in Glasgow in 1871.

Tennent Caledonian Breweries: The first bottles of Tennent's Lager rolled off the production line at the Wellpark Brewery in 1885 and they introduced canned lager in 1935.

The City of Glasgow Police, founded in 1800, was the first Police Force in Britain. However, the criminals took refuge in the Barony of Gorbals, so in 1808 the Gorbals Police Force was established.

The first turbine-driven steamer on the Clyde was the King Edward, built by Denny of Dumbarton and launched in 1901, with a top speed of over 20 knots. Her engines are on display in the Kelvingrove Art Gallery.

The Tolbooth dates from the 18th century and used to be a debtors' prison with a relaxed regime. The prisoners elected their own 'provost' and made up their own regulations, including one which said that when a prisoner was set free they would celebrate by buying all their fellow prisoners a drink!

'The Trongate, an old street, is very picturesque – high houses with an intermixture of gable fronts towards the street' was how **Dorothy Wordsworth** described it in her diary when she stayed at the Saracen's Head in August 1803. She was on her way to visit the Trossachs with her brother, the poet **William Wordsworth.**